THE WRITER'S TOOLKIT 2

how to create magical stories

by

SUE JOHNSON

Greenwood Press

First published in 2006

Greenwood Press
10 Woodward Close
Pershore
Worcs WR10 1LP

Tel: 01386 556177

Front cover illustration
Sue Johnson

ISBN: 0 9521165 4 5

Printed by

Print & Design
Worcester City Digital
2 Netherton Court
Worcester WR1 3AU

Tel: 01905 480120

CONTENTS

DEDICATION

This book is dedicated to my partner
Bob Woodroofe
with thanks for his help
with the technical stuff

to all my students
for the inspiration they give me

and also to

Vanda Inman
with thanks for her
encouragement and friendship

INTRODUCTION

So - you've got an idea for a story
and you're sitting at your desk or kitchen table
with a pile of scraps of paper
or a rough draft
wondering
'where do I go from here?'

Follow the 'Write Faster' ideas on page 9
to develop your story as much as you can.

Then look at the checklist starting on page 22.
(Use my story 'The Glass Angel' -
published in ''Take a Break: Fiction Feast'
in January 2006)
as a way of answering any questions you may have.

Remember - don't try to create and edit
at the same time.
They are two separate processes
and use different halves of the brain.

May your stories always have
a touch of magic!

WHERE DO IDEAS COME FROM?

You are your best raw material!

Start listing your childhood memories, work and travel experience – and you'll have enough material to keep you going for several years.

Carry a notebook wherever you go and use it to jot down descriptions of places and people, ideas for stories or fragments of conversation.

Try old photographs, postcards, adverts in magazines or listening to different music as a starting point.

Buy a copy of my book 'The Writer's Toolkit: banish the curse of writer's block' for further ideas.

WRITE FASTER – SWITCH OFF YOUR INTERNAL CRITIC

Most writers have a nasty little voice that comes into their head whispering "that idea's rubbish."
(Mine sounds a lot like my old English teacher!)

The following 'writing down the page' technique is one I found in 'The Weekend Novelist' by Robert Ray and Brett Norris (published by A & C Black - ISBN 0-7136-7143-2).

The trick is to write as fast as you can – using very short lines. Don't edit, punctuate or stop to find the right word. Fill as much paper as you can in the shortest possible time. Allow yourself to write badly. It doesn't have to make sense at this stage.

Writing down the page ('Glass Angel')

moaning mother
scared of wings and feathers
who does that remind you of
won't get to heaven
or be an angel
purple glass taste of blackcurrant
spiritual
spangles glass glitter
through a glass darkly
butterfly wings change things
in the amazon
start new life love drives
out fear

and so on ...

Carry on writing down the page until you have exhausted what you want to say and an idea is forming in your mind.

Use a coloured pen to mark any sections you feel will be part of the story.

When the story is clear in your mind, write a 1 – 10 plan.

<u>Sue's 1-10 Plan</u>

1. Girl meets angel
2. Mother annoyed she's late
3. More conflict
4. Girl responds differently
5. Flashback to when she bought the angel
6. The phobia about wings
7. Girl finds her feet
8. More changes
9. Mice in the attic?
10. No – bats. Exit mother

NEXT STEP

1. Write the first draft of your story.
2. Don't expect it to be perfect. First drafts are supposed to be messy. Allow your ideas to change.
3. Imagine your initial idea as a lump of clay or wood. Keep working on it until your story is the right shape.
4. Read our work aloud. You will detect any sections that don't flow smoothly.
5. Go through the checklist starting on page 22.

THE GLASS ANGEL

I never thought an angel could change my life. That was until I met one on that special Saturday in September. Let me tell you what happened.

I'd taken ages to do the shopping because of meeting the angel. Mum put on her 'nobody cares about me' look when I got home. Her bottom lip stuck out like a shelf.

"I wondered when you'd be back, Ruth."

I felt like a sixteen year old again and I reminded myself that this was my house. It was one o'clock on a Saturday lunch-time, not three o'clock in the morning. Mum didn't have to stay here if she didn't like it. She had a flat that she shared with Auntie Nora and I'd been wishing for the last two years that she'd go back there.

"Nora argues all the time," Mum said. "Besides, you need watching."

Watching was the last thing I needed, especially now I might have a new man in my life. It wouldn't be long before Mum picked up on that one and sabotaged anything before it started. She always said it was for my own good. I obviously didn't have 'the knack' with men, seeing that Ben went off with the barmaid from the 'Three Kings' two months after we got engaged.

That was two years ago. Mum moved in after a row with Auntie Nora and she'd been with me ever since, moaning about my furnishings, my food and the scratching noise in the attic.

I noticed that she'd moved the chairs again. She'd taken down the abstract painting I'd put on the wall and replaced it with a little boy in Victorian clothes with tears in his eyes. Until now, I'd have tried to ignore those things – it wasn't worth causing a fuss. Today, a different voice in my head said ' stand up to her - don't let her push you around'.

I smiled to myself. That'll be the angel I thought as I carried my bags into the kitchen.

Mum followed, limping slightly. Her bad leg always got worse when she felt someone was getting at her.

"I had to take that picture down," she said. "Them colours was giving me a headache. What've you got there? Didn't you get my tablets? What's this stuff? Garlic bread? I thought I told you to get some cheap bread from that bakers up Port Street."

"Things are changing," I said as I unwrapped the angel.

She was made of purple stained glass, edged in silver. I stood her in the kitchen window. The light radiating from her filled the kitchen.

I remembered what the man in the shop - David - said.

"They change your life. Some surprising things have happened to me since I started making Hannah and her sisters. Now they've led me to this gallery. And you."

He looked into my eyes when he said it. If it had been any other man I'd have said he was flattering me so I'd buy something. David was different.

Mum was still moaning about the bread.

"I can't eat that garlic bread. It gives me wind."

"Mum, why don't you go to the 'Three Kings' with Josie-next-door. She keeps asking you. They do a very good pensioners' lunch on a Saturday."

"I can't leave you, can I? Lord knows what you'll be up to next. Wasting your money on heaven knows what."

I swallowed my irritation.

Mum ate the garlic bread and the exotic soup I'd bought to go with it.

I smiled as I thought about David's gallery and how I never intended to go in there – until I saw the angel in the window.

It was the sort of shop Mum would dismiss as 'too posh' and 'you might break something'.

Once I was inside, I was fascinated by the patterns of light on glass. The vibrant colours spoke to me and made me feel that life could get better.

"It's never too late to change," said David, as if he read my mind.

He had eyes the colour of a summer sea and long hair in a ponytail – the sort of man that Mum would dismiss as 'arty and unreliable' before she even got to know him.

David and I talked and laughed a lot. I spent nearly two hours with him sipping coffee and looking at his collection of rainbow coloured angels.

It was magical. I could almost hear the whisper of small voices saying 'nothing will change unless you make it."

Mum didn't like the angel.

"The money you spent on that thing would've bought me a pair of shoes."

"You've got dozens of pairs in your wardrobe."

"It's not even Christmas. Besides, you know what I'm like about things with wings."

I knew all about Mum's phobia about things with wings. She couldn't stand birds, butterflies or moths. She said it made her go ‘all peculiar’ if there was anything like that within five yards of her.

“You’ll have to get used to them if you’re going to go to heaven,” I said.

There was no denying I felt different. I wasn’t going to let her grumpiness get me down any more. A voice in my head said things were changing.

For the first time in ages, I didn’t spend all weekend doing housework. On Sunday after the rain cleared, I sat in the garden watching the diamond raindrops on the grass, looking at the pattern of light on the spiders’ webs. I thought of how I always wanted to learn to paint and how Mum never encouraged that sort of thing. Now I was determined to try it.

Mum looked hostile on Monday evening when I told her I was off to join an art class.

“I’m not feeling well,” she said. “I need you here to look after me.”

“Josie-next-door’s going to look in,” I said brightly. “So you won’t be on your own.”

A few days later I sorted out my clothes. I took the old fashioned skirts and jumpers Mum liked me to wear to the charity shop. I swapped them for figure hugging jeans and silk shirts all the colours of the rainbow. I bought expensive perfume and bubble bath.

"People will get the wrong impression about you," grumbled Mum.

"They can think what they like," I said as I went out to meet David for a drink.

As I left the house I glanced at the angel and I was sure she was smiling at me.

David said he could see the angel was doing me good. I wanted to tell him it wasn't just the angel.

"The light's coming back into your life," he said as he kissed me goodnight.

"It is. It certainly is," I said as I kissed him back.

After that I started on the house. I bought velvet cushions in jewel colours - dark blue, red, acid yellow. I bought fresh flowers, candles and pot pourri.

Mum didn't like it.

"The smell of that stuff gets on my chest. You'll have to get rid of it."

I took no notice. Things had changed.

"And another thing, Ruth. You'll need to get the man from the council in. We've got mice. I can hear them scurrying in the attic. Not surprising with all that fancy stuff you keep buying."

I lay awake listening that night. It didn't sound like scurrying feet. It sounded to me like the soft movement of angels' wings.

When I got back from work today Mum was packing her bags. She'd had the man from the Council round about the mice. Except it wasn't mice. We'd got bats in our attic and they had to stay there.

"There's a preservation order on them. So we can't do nothing. And you know me with anything with wings. Makes me feel bad. I knew that angel'd bring bad luck but you wouldn't listen."

I watched as she zipped up the last suitcase.

"I've got a taxi to take me to Nora's. She hasn't got room for both of us. I don't know how you'll manage without me."

I helped her carry her bags downstairs.

Inside my head I was planning the special meal I'd cook for David tonight. My imagination felt like it had wings. I was planning how I'd convert the spare room into an art studio. I'd have stained glass windows and get David to make more angels for me.

I hoped that by the time Mum had the next argument with Auntie Nora, there would be even more changes in my life and there wouldn't be room for her to come and live here again.

As I waved her off in the taxi I thought I heard the flutter of wings behind me and the bubbling laughter of an angel.

SOME GENERAL REMINDERS

- a 'page-turning' story needs an element of conflict
- show don't tell
- show the action through the eyes of one character – don't keep skipping from one viewpoint to the other
- engage the reader's emotions
- a magazine short story only needs a very small thread of action
- keep the number of characters to a minimum
- only name important characters
- read dialogue aloud to make sure it sounds realistic
- touches of humour bring a story to life
- use the senses – sounds/smells/colours/textures so you create a full picture for the reader

CHECKLIST

Check your story

against the following points -

working through it

from beginning to end

TITLE

Does the title match the mood/atmosphere of the story?
('The Glass Angel' was one of the few times one of my titles wasn't changed by a magazine editor. My original title was 'Hannah and her Sisters' – the title of a Woody Allen film –which didn't have the same impact. (Remember there is no copyright on titles.)

Always have a working title for your story. When you're ready to send it to a magazine, ask yourself if it's the best you can think of. An intriguing title may attract an editor and is often a factor in a reader turning to your story first.

Exercise: Make a list of possible titles for stories. If you are ever stuck for an idea, pick a title and start writing.

For inspiration try The Bible, song titles, first lines of poems, old wives' tales, advertisements, nursery rhymes and fairytales.

THEME

This is the main subject of the story e.g. 'honesty is the best policy' or 'love is blind.'

Look at the captions added by the magazine. For instance - here are a few from a recent copy of 'Woman's Weekly Fiction Special' -

'love's young dream'
'a hard lesson'
'rediscovering love'
'sisters'

<u>Exercise:</u> Read a published story and see if you can work out what the theme is. Then try writing your own story using the same theme.

Make a list of your own themes - for instance:

forgiveness
revenge is sweet
jealousy
sibling rivalry
too many cooks

BEGINNINGS AND ENDINGS

The first paragraph of a story is the 'hook' that keeps your reader turning the page. It should establish the setting for the story and also give an indication of the conflict situation. Remember to start the story at a point of change for the main character.

You'll note that I've started 'The Glass Angel' at the point where Ruth has bought the angel. We don't need to know what happened before that – the argument she had with her mother over breakfast and the long wait she had for a bus etc.

End the story in such a way that the 'question' or situation posed at the beginning is answered. In this case, we don't need to know what Ruth wears on her wedding day – the fact that her mother has departed in a taxi is enough.

Exercise: **Find a photograph of a place - or use an imaginary one. Imagine a character in this place. Then write two paragraphs – the first paragraph where the person hates being there. It's raining, she can't stand the smell of wet lavender which reminds her of those miserable holidays with her aunt when she was a child…**

The second paragraph is the total opposite. The same person really loves the feel of warm sun on her bare skin and there's a beautiful sunset and somebody walking towards her with a cool glass of lager…

What you have written here is the beginning and end of a story. You've started at a point when the person is miserable because the person she loves has abandoned her. It's raining etc.

Then you fill in the middle bit…

SETTING

Setting is as important as character. The action in a story happens somewhere. Give your reader a full picture. For instance, if describing a beach scene remember to include the sound of seagulls, the smell of sun oil and seaweed, the shocking pink swimsuit worn by a small girl, the feel of cool damp sand and the taste of salt and vinegar on chips.

Make it clear to the reader where the action is taking place. Don't forget to mention that the character has moved to a different place or that time has moved on.

Setting is also historical detail, time of day and seasonal changes.

<u>Exercise:</u> Go somewhere different – a church, a café, a park – and jot down specific details about the place in your notebook. What memories or emotional feelings does it conjure up? These are important too.

Sit in a room you are familiar with. Jot down :

three objects you like
three objects you don't like
as many sounds as possible
a smell
a colour
a texture

Use this information to begin a piece of writing.

CHARACTERS

Don't make these too perfect! Show the characters in action. - don't just have an unseen narrator telling us about them.

For instance, in 'The Glass Angel', we see through Ruth's eyes how her mother behaves when she comes home with the angel.

Use flashbacks to give depth to situations and characters. Build in a few aspects of each character that are part of your own experience or memory – this will give an authentic 'feel' to the story.

Remember: SHOW DON'T TELL.

<u>Exercise:</u> Do character studies for each of your main characters – give them a birthday, a childhood and a favourite colour. What is their favourite item of clothing? What job do they do – and what is their greatest ambition or greatest fear? How do they react to stress?

Use magazine pictures or old photographs as a starting point for creating character studies.

Buy a 'babies name' book to make sure you choose names that suit your characters.

DIALOGUE

Most magazine stories are one third dialogue.

The function of dialogue is to give more information about plot and characters and to move the action of the story forward. Read dialogue aloud – cut anything that doesn't flow easily. Contract words wherever possible – e.g. 'he'd' not 'he had', 'haven't' not 'have not' 'would've' not 'would have.' (This is very useful if you need to lose a few words on a final edit).

Cut out as many 'he saids' and 'she saids' as possible. Sometimes it's stronger to use a line of action to qualify who was speaking. For instance:

> "I didn't think she'd do that."
>
> Kate turned away so Alice couldn't see the tears in her eyes.

Exercise: First write a summary – for example: 'Alice and Kate argued while they sat drinking tea in the garden.' Then write this as a scene. Show us the argument in full technicolour – how Kate flouncing in with a new handbag sparked memories of what happened all those years ago – and the boyfriend Alice lost as a result…

Which has more impact? The scene or the summary? Make sure you give your reader the full picture.

CONFLICT

Lack of conflict or dramatic tension is given as the biggest reason for the rejection of manuscripts by a number of editors.

Many writers equate conflict with writing nasty things about people.

Conflict can be:

- a difficult situation between characters
- a character's internal struggle
- a character up against the forces of nature e.g. lost in a snowstorm

An element of conflict is needed to keep the reader's interest. The reader needs to care about what happens to those people – they will quickly abandon the story if they don't!

Most magazine stories start with a person (usually female) with a problem. As the full story unfolds, she moves towards a satisfactory solution. Don't make the problem too complex. A single thread is enough - e.g what to cook her new mother-in-law for dinner not twenty years of problems with her!

Start the story at a point of change for that character.

Allow her to solve her own problems - no magic wands or knights on white chargers hurrying to the rescue.

<u>Exercise:</u> Examine three published stories and see how the writer has added dramatic tension. What was it that kept you reading to the end of the story?

How can you add more drama to your story. (Look at TV soap operas for inspiration!)

VIEWPOINT

Whose story is it? Usually it's the person with the most problems. Show us the story through the thoughts and actions of that person.

Magazine stories are usually written in first or third person.
'The Glass Angel' is written in first person. Ruth is the viewpoint character.

Third person would be if the story began: 'Ruth never thought an angel could change her life. That was until she met one that special Saturday in September…'

This story could be rewritten from the mother's viewpoint - giving a totally different perspective on the story.

Very often if you're having a problem with a story, it may be that you're trying to tell it from the wrong viewpoint. Change this and you may find it works better.

<u>Exercise:</u> Take a published story and try re-writing it from a different viewpoint. For instance, if it's a love triangle written from the wife's viewpoint – try seeing the story through the eyes of the mistress.

EMOTION

In order to make the reader want to carry on, there needs to be emotional content. If the reader doesn't care about what happens to the characters, they won't finish the story.

Don't make your characters too perfect. Show how they react when upset. Don't just say Jean was worried when her son was late home from work, show her looking anxiously out of the window, checking the television for news of any bad accidents, developing a crushing headache as she imagines the worst, fear spiralling out of control as she sees a police car go slowly past the house … and then the relief spilling over as David arrives home with a new girlfriend.

Use all the senses when writing about emotion.

Exercise: **Make a list of emotions – anger, jealousy, love, sorrow etc. Think of times in your life when you have experienced these. Write a series of short pieces detailing how you felt. Be specific. Did you feel a flash of hatred for your baby when she wouldn't stop crying – and feel like yelling at your well-intentioned mother-in-law when she offered advice? Use these emotions and feelings in your writing – it will create a ring of authenticity.**

SHAPE

The basic shape and structure of a short story is as follows:

- **an attention-grabbing opening**

- **a conflict situation** – the story should start at a point of change for the main character

- **a crisis** – this doesn't have to be a major catastrophe – burning the dinner may create sufficient tension for the characters concerned

- **the climax** – this is what the story is building towards – don't allow it to just fizzle out

- **a good ending** – allow the main character to solve his/her own problems – no lottery wins or previously unknown aunts dying and leaving loads of money

<u>Exercise:</u> Read three magazine stories carefully. See if you can identify the above elements. Make notes about the stories you have read. Have a go at creating your own stories based on those existing structures.

SENSES

Allow your reader to fully experience your story.

Show us what is happening through the eyes of your characters. How do they feel about:

- the colours of the sunset
- the feel of cool, damp sand
- the taste of salt
- the smell of vinegar on fish and chips
- the cry of seagulls wheeling overhead

Exercise: Write a detailed account of the place where you are sitting now. List how it affects all your senses. What can you hear, see, taste, smell, touch? Can you hear the mad woman next door vacuuming again? Does it make you feel irritated? Does the lingering smell of last night's curry make you remember the row you had with your boyfriend?

Aim to get this sensory detail into your stories.

FLASHBACKS

Too many flashbacks can hold up the flow of a story.

However, used in moderation, they can add depth to a character. The reader can see how the character's memory of a similar situation can influence how they choose to behave now.

When using flashback, make sure that your time shifts are clearly signposted for the reader.

If your story contains too many flashbacks, then look at the basic structure again. The beginning may need to be at an earlier point in time.

Exercise: Select three stories from different magazines and read them carefully. Look to see if flashback has been used. If so, is the switch from one time to another clear and easy to follow? How has the writer achieved this?

DOES IT SUIT YOUR PROPOSED MARKET?

Request a copy of the magazine guidelines if available.
Look at several issues of a magazine and try to get an idea of the readership it is aimed at.

For instance, if most of the advertisements are for stair lifts and fluffy slippers, you are looking at a different readership from one where the advertisements are for baby equipment and children's toys.

If you are entering a competition, read the rules carefully and make sure your story fits the criteria. If the theme is for a love story set on an English beach, don't send them a horror story set in Romania. This may sound obvious, but up to one third of competition stories are disqualified without even being read because they are too long, don't fit the required theme or arrive too late.

Remember that with magazine stories, you are allowed an extra 30 words per thousand – a story of 2000 words can actually be 2060. Always give an approximate word count when submitting to a magazine. 'Approximately 1800 words' sounds more professional than '1789'.

YOU'VE FINISHED YOUR STORY…

WHAT DO YOU DO NEXT?

1. Read it aloud to make sure it flows easily. Change any bits that don't.
2. Ensure your spelling and punctuation are correct.
3. Do a cover sheet with name, address, telephone number and approximate word count – for example 'approx 1400' looks more professional than '1387'.
4. Does your story match the guidelines given by your chosen magazine?
5. Enclose a covering letter and stamped addressed envelope for return of the manuscript if the magazine doesn't accept it.
6. Don't expect a quick reply. Some of my stories have taken six months before I've had a response. Usually, no news is good news!

REMEMBER

Look on rejection slips as part of your apprenticeship as a writer

Send a story out again as soon as possible – don't let it fester in a drawer

Be persistent

Enjoy your writing – and the journey towards publication

Reward yourself for the work you put in

The first draft

is only the beginning

of the journey ...

This is where the hard work starts ......

The writers who succeed are the ones who are prepared to rewrite and rewrite

and rewrite

until they are successful

Good luck - keep going - don't give up!

Inspiration

is

all around you

Also available from

Greenwood Press
10 Woodward Close
Pershore
Worcs WR10 1LP

Tel: 01386 556177

**'The Writer's Toolkit:
banish the curse of writer's block'
by Sue Johnson**

Tales of Trees
a collection of paired poems
by
Sue Johnson and Bob Woodroofe

A trilogy of poetry collections from
life and nature in the Vale of Evesham
by
Bob Woodroofe

**Nature of the Vale
Reflections of the Vale
Spirit of the Vale**